A New True Book

GRAND TETON

NATIONAL PARK

By David Petersen

 CHILDRENS PRESS®

CHICAGO

Autumn in the Teton Mountains

Project Editor: Fran Dyra
Design: Margrit Fiddle

Library of Congress Cataloging-in-Publication Data

Petersen, David.
  Grand Teton National Park / by David Petersen.
    p.   cm. — (A New true book)
  Includes index.
  Summary: Depicts the scenery and wildlife on view at
the Grand Teton National Park and recounts the
exploits of the area's first explorers.
  ISBN 0-516-01948-1
    1. Grand Teton National Park (Wyo.)—Juvenile
literature. [1. Grand Teton National Park (Wyo.)
2. National parks and reserves.] I. Title.
F767.T3P48   1992
917.87'55—dc20   92-9209
                                                   CIP
                                                   AC

PHOTO CREDITS
Camerique—8 (bottom)
Culver Pictures—14
© Virginia R. Grimes—22 (inset)
H. Armstrong Roberts—© D. Muench, 6 (right);
© T. Dietrich, 37; © M. Schneiders, 45
© Jerry Hennen—Cover, 24 (top & bottom right),
25 (bottom center), 44 (bottom right)
Jackson Hole Museum and Teton County
Historical Society, Jackson, Wyoming—17, 19
Grand Teton National Park—13 (right)
North Wind Picture Archives—11
PhotoEdit—© Jose Carillo, 36 (top left inset);
© Mary Kate Denny, 39 (left)
Photri—34; © MacDonald Photography, 4;
© John Robert McCauley, 22
© Branson Reynolds—6 (left), 9, 12 (3 photos),
13, 16, 21, 25 (top left & right), 31, 34 (inset),
35, 36 (bottom left & right), 38 (2 photos), 40,
43 (2 photos), 44 (left, top center, top right)
Root Resources—© Ilene MacDonald, 42 (right)
© Bob & Ira Spring—7, 29 (left)
Tom Stack & Associates—© Larry Lipsky, 26
(right); © Jeff Foott, 29 (right); © Jack D.
Swenson, 36 (top)
TSW-CLICK/Chicago—© William S. Helsel, 18;
© Paul Dix, 39 (right)
Valan—© Jean-Marie Jro, 8 (top); © J.A.
Wilkinson, 15; © Joseph R. Pearce, 23; © Jeff
Foott, 24 (left), 33, 38, 41 (right); © Wayne
Lankinen, 25 (bottom left);
© Dennis W. Schmidt, 26 (left)
Visuals Unlimited—© William Palmer, 2;
© Science VU, 41 (left)
Horizon Graphics—map, 4; diagrams, 28, 31
Cover—Grand Teton National Park

TABLE OF CONTENTS

Campsites at Signal Mountain Campground, Grand Teton National Park

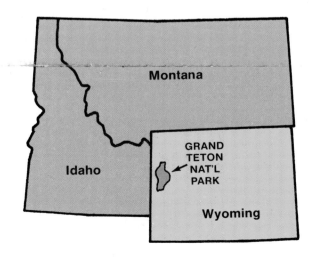

A BEAUTIFUL PLACE

In western Wyoming, near the Idaho border, is one of America's most beautiful and interesting places. It is Grand Teton National Park.

Every year, millions of people from all over the world visit this magnificent national park.

Bison—also called buffalo—(above) and moose (left) are some of the animals that live in Grand Teton park.

They come to breathe the clean air. They come to watch the wildlife. And most of all, they come to see the Teton Mountains. This range of rugged peaks is part of the Rocky Mountains.

6

The highest peak of all
is Grand Teton. It stands
13,770 feet (4,197 meters)
above sea level.

Grand Teton Mountains

Teton Village (left) lies in the beautiful green valley called Jackson Hole (below).

Jackson Hole

To the east, about 7,000 feet (2,134 meters) below the tops of the Tetons, lies a big valley called Jackson Hole. Jackson Hole is about 55 miles (89 kilometers) long and 13 miles (21 kilometers) wide. ("Hole" is the name old-time trappers gave to high mountain valleys.)

EARLY VISITORS

For thousands of years, American Indians had the Teton country all to themselves. Many tribes visited Jackson Hole during the summer months to hunt bison and other animals, to fish, and to collect roots and other

The Blackfeet came to the Teton country to hunt and fish.

plant parts. These people
included the Flathead,
Shoshone, Bannock, Crow,
Blackfeet, and Gros Ventre.
To help you learn about
these early visitors, the
park has two daily tours

A Native American park
ranger teaches a
beadwork class
at Colter Bay.

A ranger at Colter Bay Visitor Center shows visitors samples of beautiful American Indian beadwork.

to the Indian Arts Museum at Colter Bay on Jackson Lake. This place houses hundreds of pieces of American Indian clothing, crafts, and art.

Visitors can learn about other park programs at the Colter Bay Visitor Center on Jackson Lake.

EXPLORERS

John Colter

The first non-Indian to see the Tetons and Jackson Hole was a trapper named John Colter. That was in the winter of 1807-08. Colter Bay is named for him.

John Colter spread the news, and soon many trappers were coming to the Tetons in search of beaver.

Beavers were hunted for their fur.

The beaver is an animal
that has rich, brown fur. In
England, hats made from
beaver fur were popular.
That made beavers
valuable to the trappers.

In the early 1800s, some
French-Canadian trappers

South Teton, Middle Teton, and Grand Teton (left to right) make up *Les Trois Tetons*.

saw the snow-capped peaks of the Tetons for the first time. They named three of them *Les Trois Tetons* (The Three Breasts).

A little later, an American trapper named David Jackson wandered into the big valley at the foot of the Tetons. He trapped in the valley so much that his friends named it for him—Jackson Hole.

By the 1880s, farmers and ranchers were moving into Jackson Hole. They founded the town of Jackson.

This log farmhouse in Jackson Hole was built in the 1880s.

A NATIONAL PARK IS BORN

By the early 1900s, news of the wild beauty of the Teton Mountains had spread far and wide. More and more people were moving there.

But some of the new people were greedy. They wanted to develop the land for personal profit.

To protect this special place and its wildlife, the United States Congress decided to make the Teton Mountains and the lakes at their base, excluding Jackson Lake, a national park. That was in 1929.

Frank Emerson, governor of Wyoming, spoke at the dedication of Grand Teton National Park in 1929.

In 1950, the park was expanded to its present size of about 500 square miles (1,295 square kilometers). Much of the additional land was donated by a wealthy businessman named John D. Rockefeller, Jr.

The John D. Rockefeller, Jr., Memorial Parkway—a road and area of land between Grand Teton National Park and Yellowstone National Park—is named for this generous man.

Two bison cows and a calf at Grand Teton park

WILDLIFE IN GRAND TETON

The biggest wild animal
at Grand Teton park is the
bison, or buffalo. It looks
like a huge, shaggy cow.
It can weigh as much as
2,000 pounds (907 kilograms).   **21**

Winter at the National Elk Refuge. Inset: Male, or bull, elk have huge antlers.

Another wild animal found in the park is the elk, or wapiti. Elk are large deer. They like to graze in the park's wildflower-filled meadows on summer evenings.

22

In fall, the elk migrate, or move, down to the National Elk Refuge, near the town of Jackson.

A third animal you might see at Grand Teton park is the moose. Moose are the biggest deer in the world.

Moose wade in shallow rivers and ponds and eat the water plants.

Beavers cut down small trees to build dams (above).
The pika (top right) and the marmot (bottom right)
are two small animals found in the Teton country.

They can weigh as much as a thousand pounds (635 kilograms). That's as big as a horse! Moose like water, so look for them near ponds, rivers, lakes, and marshes.

Wildlife of the Teton country (clockwise from top left):
Pronghorns, bald eagle, mule deer, black bear

Other wild animals you
might be lucky enough to
see at Grand Teton park
include bears, pronghorns,
mule deer, and bald eagles.
More than 280 species
of birds live in the park in

Ospreys build nests high in treetops. Their sharp eyes can spot fish in the water far below.

the summer. One of the most interesting birds is the osprey, or "fish hawk." The osprey hovers over lakes and rivers, looking for fish swimming near the surface. When it spots a fish, it folds its wings and dives into the water to catch it.

GEOLOGY
OF THE TETONS

Geology is the study of the earth. Geologists think the Teton Mountains were formed about nine million years ago.

Before that time, the land there was flat. Pressure building within the earth caused a huge crack to open. Such cracks in the earth's crust are called faults.

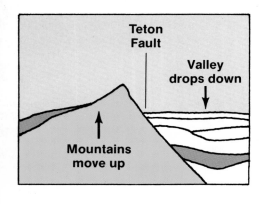

Teton Fault

Valley drops down

Mountains move up

Later fault movements caused the two sides of the fault to move in opposite directions. The land on the east side of the fault slid downward, forming the valley of Jackson Hole. The land on the west side of the fault was pushed up. This raised block of land was about 40 miles (64 kilometers) long and 15 miles (24 kilometers) wide. It was the beginning of the Teton Mountains.

Left: Winter in the Teton country. Right: A fast-flowing stream

Deep snow covered the Teton country every winter. And each spring, streams were created as the snow melted and roared down the steep eastern slope of the raised land.

29

The force of the streams gradually cut V-shaped canyons into the stony slopes.

Then came the great glaciers. A glacier is a huge mass of ice made of compressed snow. A glacier can weigh thousands of tons.

As the snow kept falling in the ancient Teton Mountains, glaciers were formed. The big, bowl-shaped depressions where the glaciers formed are

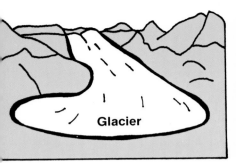

25,000 years ago

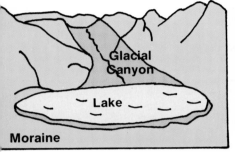

Glacial Canyon

Lake

Moraine

Today

Jenny Lake was formed when the ancient glaciers of the Tetons melted away.

called *cirques*. In the bottom of many cirques are lakes called tarns.

Tugged at by gravity, the ancient glaciers of the Tetons began slipping down the mountain canyons.

31

As the glaciers moved
slowly downward, their
hard edges scraped
against the stone.

Over thousands of years,
this constant grinding
against the sides of the
narrow, V-shaped canyons
smoothed them into wider,
U-shaped canyons.

When the climate changed
and raised the average
temperature, the glaciers
began to melt.

After the glaciers melted,

big ridges of soil and stones
that had been pushed
ahead of the glaciers
were left scattered here
and there.

Geologists call these
piles of glacial soil and
stones moraines.

Ridges of soil and stones deposited by glaciers are called moraines.

The town of Colter Bay (inset) is on Jackson Lake.
The lake was named for the trapper David Jackson.

Beautiful, clear lakes are
dotted throughout Grand
Teton National Park.
Jackson Lake is the
largest of the many

lakes found in the park.

Today, the time of the great glaciers is long past. But there are still twelve small glaciers found in the Tetons.

This small glacier is in the rugged Teton Mountains.

Camping (top), ferryboat rides
on the Snake River (left), and
stagecoach rides in the town of
Jackson (above) are some of the
fun things to do at Grand Teton park.

LOTS TO SEE AND DO

In addition to viewing the scenery and wildlife, and learning about early visitors, there are many other things to do at Grand Teton National Park.

You can camp. You can paddle a canoe on a lake. You can swim and wade.

Fishing at Oxbow Bend

Rafting on the Snake River in Grand Teton National Park. The rivers are full of fish like the cutthroat trout (inset).

You can take a trip down the Snake River. You can fish for cutthroat trout. You can hike on more than 200 miles (322 kilometers) of trails.

Hiking and horseback riding are two ways
to see the wilderness areas of the park.

Or you can ride horses
in the park. And you
can become a Young
Naturalist.

A naturalist is a person
who studies nature. The
Young Naturalists program
is designed to help you

A ranger leads a class of Young Naturalists at Moose Visitor Center.

learn about the Teton country.

To earn an official Young Naturalist badge, go to the Moose or Colter Bay Visitor Center and ask for a Young Naturalist worksheet.

The worksheet has questions about geology, wildlife, and other subjects.

Your job is to discover the answers to these questions. Look for

Beavers cut down trees with their strong front teeth (left). The alpine forget-me-not (right) is the official flower of Grand Teton park.

Signs along the trails (left) give
information about the park, and
remind visitors to respect nature.
An old log cabin (above) still stands
at Cunningham Historical Site.

answers on trailside and
roadside signs, and in
park publications. It's even
OK to ask your parents for
help.

But the fastest and most
fun way to complete your
Young Naturalist worksheet

is to participate in the park's many educational programs.

When you complete the worksheet, take it to the visitor center at Moose or Colter Bay. If your answers are

Left: A boy studies a bighorn sheep's horn at Moose Visitor Center.
Right: Demonstrating how the pioneers made cookies

Left: A Young Naturalist receives her badge. She could tell you about the trumpeter swan (above) and flowers like the Indian paintbrush (inset left) and fireweed (inset right).

correct, the ranger will award you a Young Naturalist badge.

Becoming a Young Naturalist is a great way to learn about a great place–Grand Teton National Park.

WORDS YOU SHOULD KNOW

ancient (AIN•shint)—very old; from long ago

beaver (BEE•ver)—an animal with gnawing teeth that cuts down small trees to build dams across streams

bison (BY•sun)—a large hoofed animal with short horns and a humped back; often called a buffalo

canyon (KAN•yun)—a long, narrow valley that has high cliffs on each side

cirque (SIRK)—a bowl-shaped dent, or depression, on a mountainside, caused by a glacier

cutthroat trout (KUT•throht TROUT)—a large fish that is native to the Snake River in western North America

dam (DAM)—a barrier built to hold back flowing water

depression (dih•PRESH•un)—a dent; a low place or a hollow

earthquake (ERTH•kwayk)—the shaking of the ground caused by movements of rocks deep within the earth

explorer (ex•PLOR•er)—a person who travels to an unknown place to see what is there

fault (FAWLT)—a crack or break in the earth's crust

geology (jee•AH•luh•jee)—the study of the earth

glacier (GLAY•sher)—a thick mass of ice covered with snow that moves slowly across land or down a mountain

gravity (GRAV•ih•tee)—the force that pulls and holds things down to the earth

marsh (MARSH)—low land that is covered with shallow water

meadow (MEH•doh)—a grassy area with few trees

migrate (MY•grayt)—to travel in search of better food or better weather conditions

moose (MOOSE)—a large deer with broad antlers

moraine (mor • AYN) — a hill or ridge made of gravel, rocks, and sand that was pushed ahead and finally deposited by a glacier

naturalist (NATCH • rih • list) — a person who studies nature

osprey (AHSS • pray) — a large fish-eating hawk

pronghorn (PRAWNG • horn) — a hoofed animal that looks somewhat like a deer; also called antelope

tarn (TAHRN) — a small mountain lake with steep banks

trapper (TRAP • er) — a person who catches animals for their fur

valuable (VAL • yoo • bil) — worth a lot of money

wapiti (WAH • pih • tee) — another name for an elk

wildlife (WYLD • lyf) — living things that are found in the wild; animals that are not raised by people

INDEX

About the Author

David Petersen is a full-time writer and part-time college teacher.
He lives in the Rocky Mountains of Colorado.